13-Digit ISBN: 978-1-60433-274-2
10-Digit ISBN: 1-60433-274-3

This book may be ordered by mail from the publisher. Please include $2.95 for postage and handling. Please support your local bookseller first!

Books published by Cider Mill Press Book Publishers are available at special discounts for bulk purchases in the United States by corporations, institutions, and other organizations. For more information, please contact the publisher.

Applesauce Press is an imprint of
Cider Mill Press Book Publishers
"Where good books are ready for press"
12 Port Farm Road
Kennebunkport, Maine 04046

Visit us on the Web!
www.cidermillpress.com

Design by Tilly Grassa - TGCreative Services
All illustrations courtesy of Anthony Owsley

1 2 3 4 5 6 7 8 9 0
First Edition

CONTENTS

What does a kitten use to part its fur?
A catacomb.

* * * * * * * * * * * * * *

What do you
call an old dog
that can't see?
A blind spot.

* * * * * *

LANA: I HAVE A VERY CUNNING CAT.
DONNA: WHAT MAKES YOU SAY THAT?
LANA: SHE EATS A PIECE OF CHEESE
AND THEN WAITS BY A MOUSE
HOLE WITH BAITED BREATH.

* * * * * * * * * * * * * * * * * * * *

Which holiday do dogs
like best?
Howl-o-ween.

What kind of work does a weary cat do?

Light mousework.

****

BOB: LOOK. THAT DOG IS CHASING HIS TAIL.

ROB: HE'S HAVING TROUBLE MAKING ENDS MEET.

****
What does a cat
put on a hot dog?
Moustard.

MOUSTARD

Mrs. Dog: Do you want to go to the flea market?
Mr. Dog: Yes. I'm itching to get there.

Which state has the most cats and dogs?
Petsylvania.

What kind of dog tracks
down new flowers?
A bud hound.

WHEN IS IT BAD LUCK TO HAVE A BLACK
CAT CROSS YOUR PATH?

WHEN YOU'RE A MOUSE.

* *

Don: Can I take a picture of your dog
doing a trick?
Ron: Sure. Spike will gladly be a roll
model.

Girl: Have you ever seen a catfish?
Boy: No. But I've seen a hunting dog.

• • • • • • • • • • • • • • • • • • • •

What kind of car has a motor that purrs?
A catillac.

• • • • • • • • • • • • • • • • • • • •

Judy: Where are you going in such a rush?
Rudy: I'm running away from trouble.
Judy: You can't run away from trouble. You have to face it.
Rudy: You face him. Trouble is the name of our neighbor's pit bull and here he comes!

• • • • • • • • • • • • • • • • • • • •

WHAT DOG LIVES AT A BASEBALL STADIUM?

THE CATCHER'S MUTT.

What do you get if you cross a kitten with crushed tomatoes?

Catsup.

- -

What did one cat neighbor say to the other?

Our neighborhood is going to the dogs!

Our neighborhood is going to the dogs.

- -

FIRST DOG: BARK! BARK!

SECOND DOG: MEOW! MEOW!

FIRST DOG: WHAT'S WRONG WITH YOU? A DOG DOESN'T SAY "MEOW!"

SECOND DOG: I'M LEARNING A FOREIGN LANGUAGE.

UNCLE: HOW DO YOU WAKE YOUR SON UP
        IN THE MORNING?
MOTHER: I THROW THE NEIGHBOR'S CAT
        ON HIS BED.
UNCLE: HOW DOES THAT WAKE HIM UP?
MOTHER: MY SON SLEEPS WITH HIS PET DOG.

What is the theme song of the
president's dog?
Heel to the Chief.

WHAT DO YOU GET IF YOU CROSS A
RABBIT AND TWO CATS?

HARE! KITTY! KITTY!

Boy to Girl: My pet dog
is so sophisticated he
doesn't speak. He
recites poetry
instead.

ATTENTION: K9 police make dog collars.

Why do cats climb trees? Because they don't know how to use ladders.

Why was the old dog so happy?
He had a new leash on life.

WHAT DO YOU GET IF YOU CROSS A CANTALOUPE AND LASSIE?

A MELON-COLLIE DOG.

SIGN ON AN ITCHY DOG:
Welcome to the Land of the Flea.

BOY: MY DOG IS A POLICE DOG.
GIRL: HE DOESN'T LOOK LIKE ONE.
BOY: HE'S DOING UNDERCOVER WORK.

How can you tell if a cat burglar has been in your house?
Your cat will be missing.

Knock! Knock!
Who's there?
I lecture.
I lecture who?
I lecture dog out when I came in.

Lady: I like this little dog, but I think his legs are too short.
Pet Store Clerk: They're not too short. They all reach the floor, don't they?

WHAT KIND OF PET DOES THE
ABOMINABLE SNOWMAN HAVE?

A CHILLY DOG.

**What do
you get if
you cross a
hungry cat
and a canary?
A cat that's no
longer hungry.**

Mack: How did your dog break his
front paws?
Zack: He did it burying a bone.
Mack: Really? Where?
Zack: In a parking lot.

**Which dog weighs the most?
The heavyweight boxer.**

How do you make a dog dizzy?
Give it a tail spin.

****

Boy to Girl: My pet dog is a snazzy dresser. He wears a heavy coat in winter and pants in the summer.

****

Why was Mr. Doggie late for work?
He got tied up at home.

WHERE DID THE KITTENS GO ON THEIR CLASS TRIP?

TO A SCIENCE MEWSEUM.

Girl: Why is your pet dog lying outside your front door?
Boy: He's our welcome mutt.

WHEN IS A BLOODHOUND DUMB?

WHEN HE HAS NO SCENTS.

- -

What did the weary watchdog say to his master?

I'm tired of you making me sic.

- -

Why was the little kitten so irritable?

She needed a cat nap.

They're a perfect match. He's a watchdog and she has lots of ticks.

- -

ATTENTION: DID YOU HEAR ABOUT THE DOG THAT WENT TO MEDICAL SCHOOL AND BECAME A FAMOUS HEELER?

What did the French chef say to his pet pooch at mealtime?
Bone appetite!

▲▲▲▲▲▲▲▲▲▲▲▲▲▲▲▲▲▲▲▲▲▲▲▲▲▲▲▲

What do you get if you cross a chili pepper, a gopher, and a pooch?
A hot diggity dog.

▼▼▼▼▼▼▼▼▼▼▼▼▼▼▼▼▼▼▼▼▼▼▼▼▼▼▼▼

What do you get if you cross a canine and a canary?
A doggie tweet.

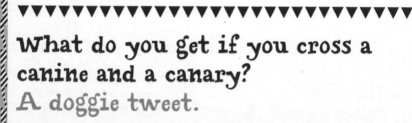

LADY: MY PET CAT HAS A LIVE BIRD IN ITS MOUTH.
VET: WHAT KIND OF BIRD?
LADY: SWALLOW.
VET: DON'T SAY THAT!

CHAPTER **2**

School Daze

Why did the clock get detention? It kept tocking in class.

WHAT SCHOOL ACTIVITY DOES JACK FROST LIKE BEST? SNOW AND TELL.

Teacher: Did your father help you with these math problems? **Student:** No, teacher. I got them wrong all by myself.

Knock! Knock!
Who's there?
Ivan.
Ivan who?
Ivan sent to the office three times today.

WHY DIDN'T THE BIOLOGY TEACHER MARRY THE PHYSICS TEACHER?

THE CHEMISTRY JUST WASN'T RIGHT.

How do bee students get to class?
They take a school buzz.

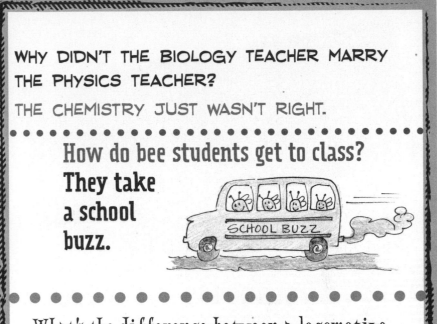

What's the difference between a locomotive engineer and a school teacher?
One minds the train and the other trains the mind.

Teacher: Our president is married to the First Lady.
Girl: I thought Adam was married to the first lady.

What do you get if you cross
a math teacher and a clock?
Arithmaticks.

What English college did the bull go to?
Oxford.

* *

KNOCK! KNOCK!

WHO'S THERE?

ALDA.

ALDA WHO?

ALDA KIDS IN MY CLASS ARE

TALLER THAN ME.

* *

**How does a gym teacher keep
evil spirits out of the gym?**
He exorcises them.

Gym Teacher: What is your favorite aquatic sport?
Student: Channel surfing.

* * * * * * * * * * * * * * * * * * * *

WHAT'S THE FIRST
CLASS A SNAKE
TAKES IN SCHOOL?
HISSTORY.

Cara: Basket-making class is cancelled.
Lara: Why?
Cara: The teacher took a weave of absence.

Why did the farmer take a math class?
He wanted to learn about square roots.

STUDENT: DO YOU HAVE ANY BOOKS ON GAMBLING CASINOS?

LIBRARIAN: YOU BET WE DO.

Jack: I read a book on how they made the Holland and Lincoln tunnels.
Mack: Boring!

Boy: Summer vacation is getting to be too short.
Girl: What do you mean?
Boy: It's not long enough for me to forget what I learned in school all year.

Girl: I want to take my college classes on a cruise ship.
Advisor: First you have to go to boarding school.

FATHER: DID YOUR CHEMISTRY TEACHER LIKE YOUR CLASS PROJECT?
BOY: HE LOVED IT. IN FACT, IT BLEW HIM AWAY.

What flies around a kindergarten class at night?
The alphabat.

Boy: My teacher talks to herself.
Father: Does she know that?
Boy: Nah. She thinks we're listening to her.

TEACHER: TODAY WE'RE HAVING AN I.Q. TEST.
DORK: OH NO! I FORGOT TO STUDY FOR IT.

What did the astronaut give the school bully?
His launch money.

WHY DIDN'T 2 GO OUT WITH 3?
HE WAS A LITTLE ODD.

"Hi!"

SIGN IN GYM: Watch your step. No class trips.

Girl: What are you reading?
Boy: A mystery.
Girl: But that's a math textbook.
Boy: It's a mystery to me.

Grandfather: How could you do so badly in history? I always excelled in this class.
Grandson: That's because there was less history to study when you were in school.

What was the name of the Quiz Kid's father?
Pop Quiz.

WHO'S THE SMARTEST PUPIL IN THE ALPHABET?

THE A STUDENT.

Who's the saddest letter in the alphabet?

The blue J.

Which two letters of the alphabet announce who the smartest pupil in your class is?

I-M. ***********************

Jack: My teacher always picks on me and makes fun of me.

Mack: So transfer to another class.

Jack: I can't. I'm home schooled.

WHAT DO YOU NEED TO PASS MED SCHOOL?

LOTS OF PATIENTS.

****

KNOCK! KNOCK!

WHO'S THERE?

ADOPT.

ADOPT WHO?

ADOPT MY PEN ON THE FLOOR AND IT ROLLED AWAY.

Bill: Did you climb the ropes in gym?
Will: Yes. For a few minutes I was alone at the top of my class.

• • • • • • • • • • • • • • • • •

Gym Teacher: Tomorrow we're going to jump rope.
Girl: Yahoo! I finally get to skip class.

* * * * * * * * * * * * * *

WHAT CLASS DOES MR. SODA POP TEACH?

FIZZ ED.

* *

Why did the geek take his report to the school dance?
The teacher told him to date his paper.

Why did the dentist go back to medical school?
He wanted to brush up on his studies.

- - - - - - - - - - - - - - - - - - - -

What did the fish give his teacher?
A crabapple.

- - - - - - - - - - - - - - - - - - - -

JENNY: WHY DID YOU DROP OUT OF MEDICAL SCHOOL?

LENNY: I'M SICK OF DOING HOMEWORK.

- - - - - - - - - - - - - - - - - - - -

Then there was the large math teacher who wore plus-size clothes.

$$2 + 2 = \underline{}$$
$$3 + 2 = \underline{}$$

Ted: I got an "A" for cutting class.

Fred: What? How's that possible?

Ted: I go to barber school.

• •

WHAT DO YOU USE TO CATCH A SCHOOL OF FISH?

BOOKWORMS.

• •

Knock! Knock!
Who's there?
Anita.
Anita who?
Anita borrow a pencil.

• •

What do band students sit on?
Musical chairs.

Why did the girl get a bad grade in cooking class? Her dog ate her homework.

* * * * * * * * * * * * * *

WHAT DO YOU CALL A TEACHER'S ASSISTANT WHO'S FROM ANOTHER COUNTRY?

FOREIGN AIDE.

****

Teacher Sez: Today we're going to study about growing a garden. Take out your weeding books.

What do you call a part-time music instructor who gives trumpet lessons?
A substi-toot teacher.

TEACHER: **WHAT DO YOU LIKE BEST ABOUT BAKERY SCHOOL?**
STUDENT: **ROLL CALL.**

* * * * * * * * * * * * * *

Why was the student
sheep so sad?
She flunked her
baaology test.

* * * * * * * * * * * * * * * * * * *

BOY: DAD, I THINK OUR TRACK TEAM IS
GOING TO LOOSE..
DAD: WHAT MAKES YOU SAY THAT?
BOY: ON THE ROAD THAT LEADS TO THE
BUILDING THERE'S A SIGN THAT READS,
"SLOW SCHOOL AHEAD."

* * * * * * * * * * * * *

**Hal: We're all going to join the
school math club.
Cal: Well, count me out.**

KNOCK! KNOCK!
WHO'S THERE?
WEIRD.
WEIRD WHO?
WEIRD YOU GET THE ANSWERS TO
THIS TEST?

* *

What kind of book should you bring to music class?

A note pad.

What did the math student say to the algebra problem?

I just can't figure you out.

* *

What did the math student say to the geometry teacher?

You know all the angles!

Why did the young teacher take diving lessons? He wanted to work as a sub.

MR. JOHNSON

Teacher: In order for their species to survive, animals must breed.
Student: Duh! If animals didn't breed, they'd suffocate.

SOME SILLY TEACHERS:
MR. MARK R. EXAMS
MS. KIM S. TREE
MR. M. T. HALLS
MR. TEX BOOKER
MR. HUGH FLUNK

Why was the astronaut absent during lunch?
He forgot his launchbox.

What has feathers and
gives yearly physicals?
The school ducktor.

What happened to Miss
Cherry?
She graduated at the top of
her sundae school class.

Knock! Knock!
Who's there?
Chauffeur.
Chauffeur who?
**Chauffeur this semester I've
received two As and a B.**

TEACHER: WHAT ARE THE THREE WORDS
I NEVER WANT TO HEAR SPOKEN
IN MY CLASS?
STUDENT: I DON'T KNOW.
TEACHER: THAT'S CORRECT.

- -

Millie: I went to school to learn
how to shop better.
Tillie: What did you study?
Millie: Buyology.

● ●

WILLIE: I'M GOING TO CLOWN COLLEGE.
NILLY: DID YOU GET A FOOL
SCHOLARSHIP?

● ● ● ● ● ● ● ● ● ● ● ● ● ● ●

**What should you give
a drum majorette who
skins her knee?
Band-aid.**

Bessie: What do the students do at Clown College?

Tessie: We just fool around.

How do you get to be a cosmetologist?
Take a makeup test.

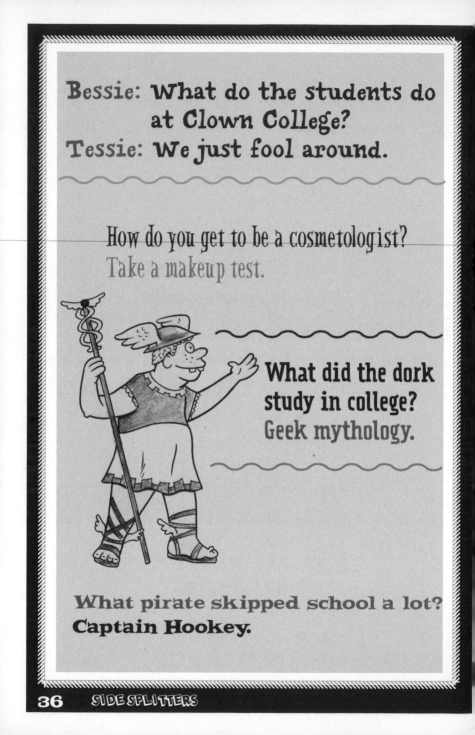

What did the dork study in college?
Geek mythology.

What pirate skipped school a lot?
Captain Hookey.

CHAPTER
3
Zingers

I BET YOU GO TO THE DENTIST TWICE A YEAR. ONCE FOR EACH TOOTH.

▲▲▲▲▲▲▲▲▲▲▲▲▲▲▲▲▲▲▲▲▲▲▲▲▲▲▲▲▲▲▲

Aunt Bertha: How much do you weigh, Joey?

Joey: About a hundred pounds.

Aunt Bertha: I remember when I weighed a hundred pounds.

Joey: Gosh, you have a good memory.

▼▼▼▼▼▼▼▼▼▼▼▼▼▼▼▼▼▼▼▼▼▼▼▼▼▼▼▼▼

GIRLS DON'T CLOSE THEIR EYES WHEN THEY KISS YOU. YOU HAVE TO BLINDFOLD THEM.

▼▼▼▼▼▼▼▼▼▼▼▼▼▼▼▼▼▼▼▼▼▼▼▼▼▼▼▼▼▼

If looks could kill, a glance at your face would be fatal.

You act like a big shot, but your mind is a blank.

▲▲▲▲▲▲▲▲▲▲▲▲▲▲▲▲▲▲▲▲▲▲▲▲▲▲▲

There's something heavenly about you. People look at your face and shout, "Oh, God!"

▼▼▼▼▼▼▼▼▼▼▼▼▼▼▼▼▼▼▼▼▼▼▼▼▼▼▼▼

Wife: Golf! Golf! Golf! I think if you spent one whole weekend at home, I'd drop dead.
Husband: Don't say that, dear. You know you can't bribe me.

Writer: Do you think I should put more fire into my new novel?
Agent: No. I think you should put your new novel into the fire.

Ben: Do you want to see me do a magic trick?
Jen: Only if you promise to disappear.

Lady: Do you call that hideous thing modern art?
Artist: No. I call it a mirror.

His hair is so greasy, lice only visit his head when they want to go skiing.

HE HAS SO MUCH DANDRUFF, THE FLEAS LIVE ON HIS HEAD IN BLIZZARD CONDITIONS.

We'd like a breath of fresh air, so do us a favor and hold yours.

She's so boring she couldn't be the life of the party at a zombie convention.

HE'S SUCH A BLOCKHEAD HE DOESN'T GET DANDRUFF. HE GETS SAWDUST.

Is it true elephants never forget or do you have trouble remembering certain things?

Okay tough guy. I admit that you're stronger than I am. But bad breath isn't everything.

You're in a bad mood today. What did you do? Get up on the wrong side of your cage this morning?

A STORK DIDN'T DELIVER YOU TO THE MATERNITY WARD. IT WAS A VULTURE.

Grandmother: **When I was growing up everybody was a gentleman.**
Granddaughter: **You mean you were the only woman on earth, Granny?**

Your grandfather is so old he knew Hercules when he was a 98-pound weakling.

Your uncle is so old he sold Noah flood insurance.

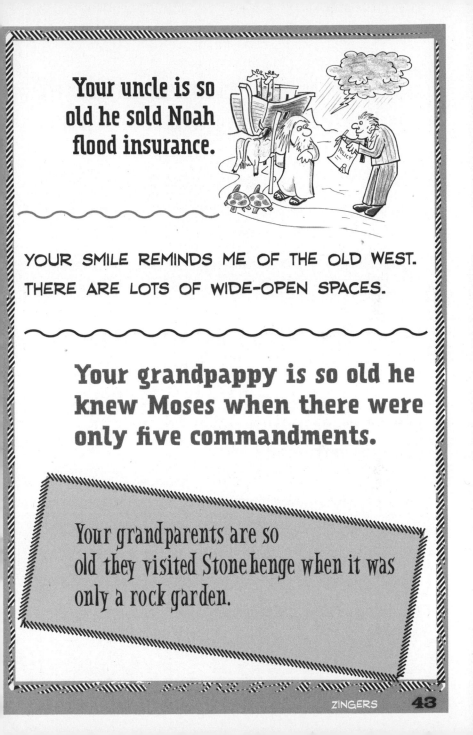

YOUR SMILE REMINDS ME OF THE OLD WEST. THERE ARE LOTS OF WIDE-OPEN SPACES.

Your grandpappy is so old he knew Moses when there were only five commandments.

Your grandparents are so old they visited Stonehenge when it was only a rock garden.

Lady: I have the face of an eighteen-year-old girl.
Man: Give it back. You're getting it all wrinkled.

* * * * * * * * * * * * * * *

YOUR GRANDPARENTS ARE SO OLD THEY
JUMPED ACROSS THE GRAND CANYON
WHEN IT WAS ONLY A MUDDY DITCH.

Grandfather: When I was your age I could name all of the U.S Presidents in order.
Boy: Big deal! How hard is it to remember George Washington, John Adams and Thomas Jefferson?

* *

Your grandparents are so old they traveled through the forest when the Giant Redwoods were just saplings.

Millie: I just spent two hours in front of a mirror admiring my beauty. Is that vanity?
Tillie: No. Imagination.

OH, BY THE WAY. SASQUATCH CALLED, HE WANTS HIS FEET BACK.

You have a sympathetic face. Everyone who sees it feels sorry for you.

* * * * * * * * * * * * *

A lot of exercise is good for a person. Your tongue must be in great shape.

* *

There's only one trouble with your face: it shows.

She's so homely, she had a coming-out party and then they made her go back in again.

● ●

When you were born, people came from miles around to see you. And everyone asked the same question. What is it?

● ●

The last time he walked through a circus sideshow the freaks gave him a standing ovation.

● ●

BOYFRIEND: DID YOU LIKE THE BIRTHDAY GIFT I GAVE YOU?

GIRLFRIEND: YES. I CAN'T WAIT TO EXCHANGE IT.

Why don't you join your boyfriend for dinner tonight? Feeding time at the zoo is at 6:00.

• •

Hey, Halloween is over. Take off your mask.

• •

She has to go to the beauty parlor two days in a row. The first day is to get an estimate.

• • • • • • • • • • • • • • • • • • • •

He has a baby face and an infantile brain.

• • • • • • • • • • •

IF DR. FRANKENSTEIN REMOVED YOUR BRAIN, HE COULD CARRY IT HOME IN A THIMBLE.

His brain cells are filled with inmates convicted of criminal stupidity.

I finally figured out why you always have that silly grin on your face. You're just naturally silly.

When she sends out brainwaves, they're microwaves.

A fortuneteller read her mind. It was a very short story.

Her hair is so frizzy the hairdresser doesn't cut it ... she prunes it.

I'M NOT SAYING YOU'RE A TURKEY, BUT HOW DO YOU MANAGE TO SURVIVE EVERY THANKSGIVING.

Your stomach may be rumbling, but it's your brain that's out to lunch.

You're so weak you couldn't bend licorice.

He's a guy who is rock solid, especially his head.

* * * * * * * * * *

You should become a bone specialist.

You've got the head for it.

She's like the statue of Venus de Milo—beautiful, but not all there.

SHE HAS A PRETTY LITTLE HEAD AND A BRAIN THAT'S PRETTY LITTLE TOO.

I heard you had plastic surgery to improve your looks. How's the malpractice suit going?

* *

Everyone is rooting for her to get ahead. The one she already has is useless.

THE LAST TIME I SAW EARS AS BIG AS YOURS THEY WERE ON A CORNSTALK.

She's so boring people with insomnia invite her over to put them to sleep.

He hasn't seen his twin brother in so long; he's forgotten what he looks like.

Your brain is like a lost roll of film. It was never developed.

She's so silly she brought a bar of soap to a bridal shower.

He had a headache so he went to a doctor to have his brain examined. The doctor found nothing.

She's so clue-less she thinks you have to stand on your head to bake an upside-down cake.

HE'S SO SILLY HE THINKS THE
KENTUCKY DERBY IS A HAT.

HE HAD HIS BRAIN CHECKED OUT
WHEN HE WAS YOUNG, AND IT NEVER
CHECKED BACK IN.

My doctor told me to
exercise with dumbbells so
I came by to invite you and
your brother to jog with me.

He's getting a B.A. degree. He
finally mastered the first two
letters of the alphabet even
though he got them backwards.

CHAPTER **4**
Monster Mayhem

Monster 1: I just devoured a gym teacher, a fitness expert, and an aerobics instructor.

Monster 2: Gosh! You sure eat a lot of health food.

- -

Where do you go to gas up a monster truck?
To a villain station.

- -

MONSTER 1: LAST NIGHT I HAD MY NEW NEIGHBORS FOR DINNER.

MONSTER 2: HOW WAS THE MEAL?

MONSTER 1: GREAT! THEY WERE DELICIOUS.

- -

Which dinosaur likes to play golf?
Tee Rex.

Why does Frankenstein walk funny?
Monster wedgie.

* *

WHY DID THE FRANKENSTEIN MONSTER GO TO A PSYCHIATRIST?

HE THOUGHT HE HAD A SCREW LOOSE.

Why did Dr. Cyclops close his ophthalmology school?

He only had one pupil.

Who is spooky and lives under the sea?
Sponge Blob Scare Pants.

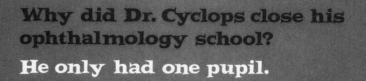

NOTICE: BIG FOOT DRIVES A MONSTER TOE TRUCK.

What do you do with a
blue monster?
Cheer it up.

* * * * * * * *

What did Godzilla
say when he saw a
NASCAR race?
Oh boy! Fast food.

Why did the Invisible Woman go to the
beauty parlor?
Her hair had no body at all.

What's ghastly and cleans floor?
The Grim Sweeper.

* *

Who haunts the chicken coop?
The Grim Peeper.

▲▲▲▲▲▲▲▲▲▲▲▲▲▲▲▲▲▲▲▲▲▲▲▲▲▲▲▲▲▲▲▲▲

Igor: Where did you learn to write horror stories?
Boris: In a little red ghoul house.

▼▼▼▼▼▼▼▼▼▼▼▼▼▼▼▼▼▼▼▼▼▼▼▼▼▼▼▼▼▼▼▼▼

WHY DID BABY FRANKENSTEIN ASK SO
MANY QUESTIONS?
AFTER THE MAD DOCTOR CHARGED
HIM UP, HE WAS FULL OF WATTS.

▲▲▲▲▲▲▲▲▲▲▲▲▲▲▲▲▲▲▲▲▲▲▲▲▲▲▲▲▲▲▲▲▲

Why did Little Frankenstein
go to the playground?
He wanted to ride the
scary-go-round.

Artifact Dealer: Would you like to purchase an Egyptian mummy? Customer: Yes. And could you gift-wrap it?

▼▼▼▼▼▼▼▼▼▼▼▼▼▼▼▼

WHY DOESN'T DEATH EVER MISS A PHONE CALL?

HE HAS A GRIM BEEPER.

▲▲▲▲▲▲▲▲▲▲▲▲▲▲▲▲▲▲▲▲▲▲▲▲▲▲▲▲▲

Who cleans up a dirty dungeon?
The torture chambermaid.

▼▼▼▼▼▼▼▼▼▼▼▼▼▼▼▼▼▼▼▼▼▼▼

Why did Godzilla devour the Eiffel Tower?
He was in the mood for French food.

Ivan: We'll have to do something about the hot-tempered monster you created.
Mad Doctor: Why?
Ivan: It keeps losing its head.

Why did Godzilla eat a volcano?

He wanted a hot lunch.

MAD DOCTOR: HOW CAN I CREATE MONSTERS IF I HAVE NO PARTS TO WORK WITH?
BORIS: DON'T BLAME ME IF YOU'RE HAVING AN OUT-OF-BODIES EXPERIENCE.

Where does the Abominable Snowman hide his secret money?
In a slush fund.

What did the yeti say when he found a frozen Roman soldier?
Oh boy! Italian ice.

Why did Godzilla eat the burning apartment building?
He likes home cooking.

What did Godzilla say after he ate a dozen armored vehicles?
Tanks for dinner.

Why did Godzilla eat Fort Knox?
He wanted an after-dinner mint.

* * * * * * * * * * * * * *

WHERE DO MONSTERS GO TO BUY A USED CAR?
IN THE BORIS CAR LOT.

* *

What creature did Mad Dr. Cheese invent?
The Frankenstein Muenster.

What does the Frankenstein Monster do when he runs short of energy?
He uses his monster charge card.

MAD DOCTOR: YESTERDAY I CREATED A ROPE MONSTER.

IGOR: DID KNOT!

* * * * * * * *

Monster: My fingers don't work right.

Mad Scientist: I knew I shouldn't have used second-hand parts when I made you.

Vampire: Hello, stranger. Where are you from?

Frankenstein Monster: Parts of me are from New York, Texas, Ohio, Maine, Alabama, New Jersey, and other places.

Vampire: Wow, you're a real all-American guy.

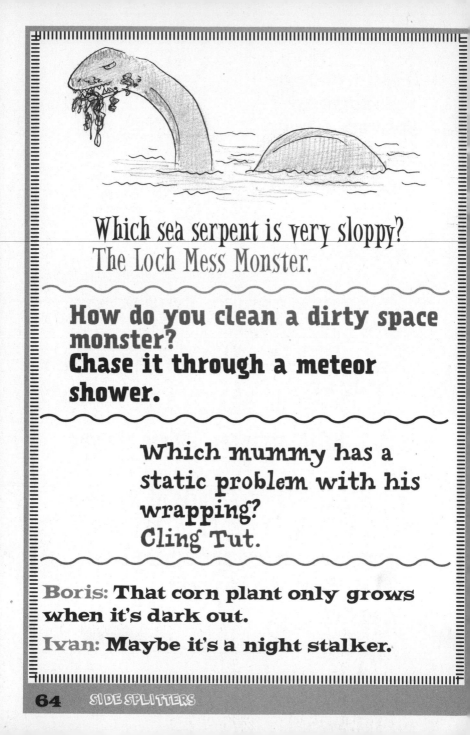

Which sea serpent is very sloppy?
The Loch Mess Monster.

How do you clean a dirty space monster?
Chase it through a meteor shower.

Which mummy has a static problem with his wrapping?
Cling Tut.

Boris: That corn plant only grows when it's dark out.

Ivan: Maybe it's a night stalker.

MAD SCIENTIST: I PLAN TO CREATE A GIANT RABBIT MONSTER.

IGOR: HUMPH! NOW THAT'S A HARE-BRAINED SCHEME.

What kind of vegetables do monsters eat?
Human beans.

How do you make a gingerbread monster?
Use weird dough.

MAD MENU NOTICES:
GODZILLA EATS REAL SUBMARINE SANDWICHES.

VAMPIRES HATE STAKE DINNERS.

What do you get if you cross a Sasquatch with a centipede.

A big foot, foot, foot, foot, foot, foot.

● ●

MONSTER #1: GRR! I'M REALLY ANGRY. THE MAD DOCTOR WHO CREATED ME FORGOT TO GIVE ME A BRAIN TRANSPLANT.

MONSTER #2: CALM DOWN AND I'LL GIVE YOU A PIECE OF MY MIND.

● ● ● ● ● ● ● ● ● ● ●

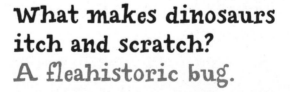

Which dinosaur loves to wear plaid clothing? Tyrannosaurus Chex.

● ● ● ● ● ● ● ● ● ● ● ● ● ●

What makes dinosaurs itch and scratch?

A fleahistoric bug.

WHO IS THE BIGGEST DINOSAUR CROOK?

THE GANGSTA' RAPTOR.

· ·

What do you get if you cross a wild horse with a dinosaur?
A Broncosaurus.

· ·

**Yeti: Did you date the Abominable Snowgirl?
Sasquatch: No. I asked her out, but she gave me the cold shoulder.**

· ·

Where's the best place for a mummy to live?
In an old, old, old, old, old age home.

What does BFF mean
to a monster?
Beast Friends Forever.

* * * * * * * * * * * *

What kind of novels does the
Abominable Snowman write?
Chilling tales of suspense.

**What does a yeti grow
in his Himalayan garden?
Llama beans.**

DRACULA: I'LL SEE YOU LATER.
INVISIBLE MAN: NO YOU WON'T.

What do you put on a zombie wanted poster?
Wanted Dead or Not Alive.

Where does a zombie keep a skeleton bird?

In a rib cage.

WHAT DO YOU CALL DRACULA'S UNRULY CHILDREN?

VAMPIRE BRATS.

Mad Dr. Morgon: My new monster stands ten feet tall. I named the creature "If."

Gorgon: Gosh! That's a mighty big if.

How does a silly monster count up to fifteen?
It uses its fingers.

▲▲▲▲▲▲▲▲▲▲▲▲▲▲▲▲▲▲▲▲▲▲▲▲▲▲▲▲▲▲▲

What happened when the angry villagers trapped the monster orange?
They beat it to a pulp!

▼▼▼▼▼▼▼▼▼▼▼▼▼▼▼▼▼▼▼▼▼▼▼▼▼▼▼▼▼▼▼

What's the best way to view a horror movie?
Watch it on a wide-scream TV.

▲▲▲▲▲▲▲▲▲▲▲▲▲▲▲▲▲▲▲▲▲▲▲▲▲▲▲▲▲▲▲

Why didn't the mummy take a vacation?
He was wrapped up in his work.

What does a yeti ride?
An Abominable Snowmobile.

▲▲▲▲▲▲▲▲▲▲▲▲▲▲▲▲▲▲▲▲▲▲▲▲▲▲▲▲▲

WHAT DID THE EVIL MUMMY SAY AFTER THEY WRAPPED HIM IN ALUMINUM?

CURSES! FOILED AGAIN!

▼▼▼▼▼▼▼▼▼▼▼▼▼▼▼▼▼▼▼▼▼▼▼▼▼▼▼▼▼

What giant ape writes horror stories? Stephen King Kong.

▲▲▲▲▲▲▲▲▲▲▲▲▲▲▲▲▲▲▲▲▲▲▲▲▲▲▲▲▲

INVISIBLE MAN: WHY WON'T YOU GIVE ME THE LEAD ROLE IN YOUR NEW HORROR MOVIE?
DIRECTOR: SORRY, BUT I JUST CAN'T SEE YOU IN THE PART.

* * * * * * * * * * * * * * *

Did you hear about the sea monster that had whale-to-whale carpeting in his house?

Where do baby monsters stay while their parents work? At dayscare centers.

* * * * * * * * * * * * * * *

MAD DOCTOR: I MADE A MONSTER OUT OF AN OLD LOCOMOTIVE. IT HAS A HEAD FULL OF STEAM.

IGOR: DON'T FORGET TO ATTACH ITS ENGINE EARS.

How did the fortune teller predict the monster's future?
She checked his horrorscope.

Why are you at the hospital?

Vampire: I need a blood transfusion.

Mr. Zombie: I'm stiff all over.

Mr. Skeleton: I have a fractured bone.

The Invisible Man: I need to clear up my complexion.

Mrs. Devil: I'm having hot flashes.

Abominable Snowman: I have cold feet.

Werewolf: I'm shedding.

Ms. Witch: I'm having fainting spells.

* * * * * * * * * * * * * *

Mad Doctor: I want to dissect this bee monster.

Igor: I'll get the buzz saw.

What's scary, hairy and slides down an icy slope real fast? A yeti on a snowboard.

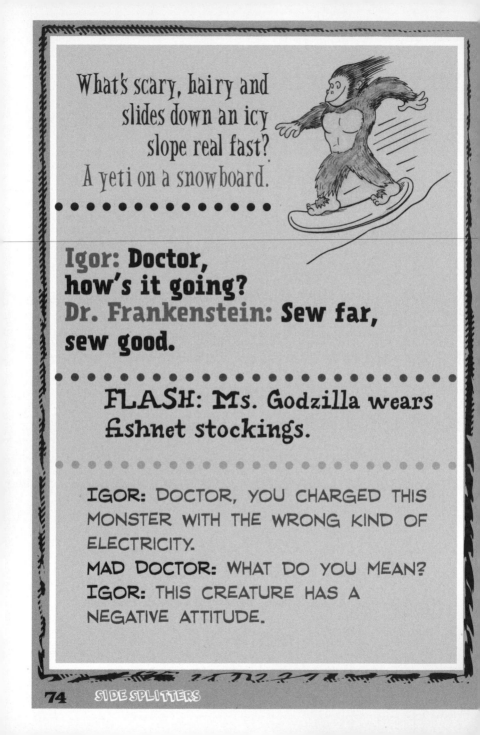

• • • • • • • • • • •

Igor: **Doctor, how's it going?**
Dr. Frankenstein: **Sew far, sew good.**

• • • • • • • • • • • • • • • • •

FLASH: Ms. Godzilla wears fishnet stockings.

• • • • • • • • • • • • • • • • •

IGOR: DOCTOR, YOU CHARGED THIS MONSTER WITH THE WRONG KIND OF ELECTRICITY.
MAD DOCTOR: WHAT DO YOU MEAN?
IGOR: THIS CREATURE HAS A NEGATIVE ATTITUDE.

What did the Egyptian mummy say to the river?

Nile see you later.

● ●

MAD DOCTOR: *SUCCESS AT LAST! MY APPLE MONSTER IS ALIVE AND IT'S ROTTEN TO THE CORE!*

● ●

What do you call the mother and father of invisible children?

Transparents.

● ●

Divorce lawyer: **Why are you here, Mrs. Frankenstein?**

Mrs. Frankenstein: **My marriage to the Mad Doctor was an experiment that failed.**

WHAT KIND OF MUSIC DO
SPACE MONSTERS LIKE?
MOON ROCK.

What did Dr. Frankenstein say
to the three-legged monster?

You've grown a foot since I last saw you.

****

**Who won the skeleton
beauty contest?**

No body.

****

What does the
Abominable
Snowman get
when he eats ice
cream too fast?
Brain freeze.

CHAPTER **5**

Loony Law & Order

Lawyer #1: Mr. Rabbit, will you please tell the court what Mrs. Bunny said to you.

Lawyer #2: Objection, your honor. Haresay.

* * * * * * * * * *

What did the detective say when he arrested a mime? You have the right to remain silent.

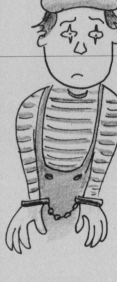

* * * * * * * * * *

Annette: How's your job at the law office?

Jeannette: Every day it's a test of wills.

* * * * * * * * * * * * * * *

ACCUSED: I PLEAD INSANITY, YOUR HONOR.

JUDGE: YOU'RE OUT OF YOUR MIND.

ACCUSED: THANKS FOR ALLOWING MY DEFENSE, JUDGE.

Knock! Knock!
Who's there?
We flounder.
We flounder who?
We flounder innocent of
all charges.

* * * * * * * * * * * * * * *

Judge: Counselor, where is your client?

Magician's lawyer: I expect him to appear before you any second now.

* * * * * * *

HOW DO YOU
CONTACT A CONVICT
IN JAIL?
CALL HIM ON HIS
CELL PHONE.

WHAT'S THAT?
PRINCE ALBERT IN
THE CAN? MY
REFRIGERATOR ON
THE RUN?
WHO IS THIS?!

* * * * * * * * * *

Who proofreads
all manuscripts
written by jailhouse authors?
The corrections officer.

Why is a judge like a reserve baseball player?
They both spend a lot of time on the bench.

Lawyer: Whenever I stand up in court to speak to the judge, I suddenly feel ill. What's wrong with me?
Doctor: It sounds like motion sickness to me.

Why did the lawyer bring a mattress to court?
He was about to rest his case.

COP: I JUST SAW A KID FISHING FROM A RAILROAD BRIDGE OVER THE RIVER.
DETECTIVE: ARREST HIM. OFF TRACK BAITING IS ILLEGAL IN THIS STATE.

You're under arrest!

DAFFY DEFINITION:
American Robbers, Inc. –
a U.S. steal company.

What did the sheep
thief do after
the robbery?
She took it
on the lamb.

WHAT DID THE DETECTIVE SAY TO
HIS SHIRT?
YOU'RE UNDER A VEST!

Why did the cop give the hog
a ticket?
Because he went through a
slop sign.

What do you call a bunch of crooks playing musical instruments?
A robber band.

NUTTY LEGAL NAMES
Mr. Scott Free
Mr. Carl D. Witness
Mr. Al Stan Trial
Mr. Otto Order
Ms. I.M. Innocent
Mr. Mike A. Motion
Mr. Ken Hugh Postbale
Mr. Howe Dewey Plead

Lawyer: Your honor, my client is accused of stealing a dead car battery.
Judge: In that case I guess they'll be no charges.

SINGER: I DID A BENEFIT SHOW AT THE PRISON.
REPORTER: HOW WAS THE CROWD?
SINGER: THEY WERE A CAPTIVE AUDIENCE.

What do you find on the front of a gangster's limo?

A hood ornament.

▲▲▲▲▲▲▲▲▲▲▲▲▲▲▲▲▲▲▲▲▲▲▲▲▲▲▲▲▲▲

WHAT DO YOU GET WHEN A MESSY CROOK SPREADS DIRT EVERYWHERE?

A GRIME SCENE.

▼▼▼▼▼▼▼▼▼▼▼▼▼

Then there was the jailhouse spoon who went stir crazy.

Knock! Knock!
Who's there?
Veer.
Veer who?
Veer were you Friday night
at ten o'clock?

Why did the Energizer Bunny spend a night in jail?
It was a case of battery.

When is it illegal for a cat to fall asleep?
When it's a case of kit napping.

WHY DID THE OCTOPUS GO TO PRISON?
IT WAS GUILTY OF ARMED, ARMED ROBBERY.

KNOCK! KNOCK!
WHO'S THERE?
PEAR.
PEAR WHO?
PEAR-JURY IS A SERIOUS OFFENSE.

What did the poker player say to the District Attorney?
Give me a good deal.

Why did the judge climb Mt. Everest?
He wanted to preside over the highest court in the land.

Why did the lawyer yell in court?
He wanted to make sure his case was heard.

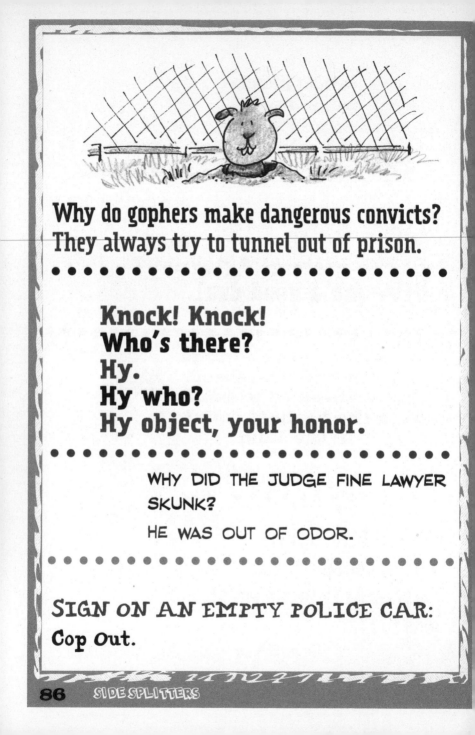

Why do gophers make dangerous convicts?
They always try to tunnel out of prison.

● ●

Knock! Knock!
Who's there?
Hy.
Hy who?
Hy object, your honor.

● ● ● ● ● ● ● ● ● ● ● ● ● ● ● ● ● ● ● ●

WHY DID THE JUDGE FINE LAWYER
SKUNK?

HE WAS OUT OF ODOR.

● ● ● ● ● ● ● ● ● ● ● ● ● ● ● ● ● ● ● ●

SIGN ON AN EMPTY POLICE CAR:
Cop Out.

Why did the jail inmate put a clock in the stew?
Because the warden ordered him to serve time in the prison kitchen.

• •

WHY DO YOU SELDOM SEE CROOKS IN CHURCH?

BECAUSE CRIME DOESN'T PRAY.

• •

What is Detective Polar Bear great at solving?

Cold cases.

• •

Police Chief:
Did you arrest the banana thief?
Detective:
No. He gave me the slip.

• • • • • • • • • • • • •

Knock! Knock!
Who's there?
Police.
Police who?
Police don't arrest me. I didn't do anything.

BUSTER: CRIME IS REALLY BAD IN MY NEIGHBORHOOD. ON CHRISTMAS EVE SANTA CLAUS COMES DOWN THE CHIMNEY WEARING A RED SUIT AND A MATCHING SKI MASK.

LESTER: CRIME IS SO BAD IN MY NEIGHBORHOOD A BANK ROBBER WAS MUGGED RACING TO HIS GETAWAY CAR.

Desk Sergeant: Why are you so upset because someone stole your new pair of shoes?
Victim: They were my sole support.

Victim: A crime has been committed. Quick. Call 9-1-1!
Witness: Okay. What's the number?

What did the meter maid
give the pig?
A porking ticket.

* * * * * * * * *

Why did the
detective give the
crime boss an ant farm?
He wanted to bug his office.

* * * * * * * * * * * * * *

WHAT DID MR. BARTLETT SHOUT IN
COURT?
I WANT TO BE JUDGED BY A JURY OF
MY PEARS.

How do you safeguard a
boneheaded informant?
Put him in the witless protection
program.

Knock! Knock!
Who's there?
Karma.
Karma who?
Karma out with your hands up.

* * * * * * * * * * * * * *

What kind of a weapon does a gangster tuck in his belt? A tummy gun.

* * * * * * *

WHAT HAPPENED TO THE CROOKED LIBRARIAN?

THE JUDGE THREW THE BOOK AT HER.

* *

Then there was the antelope convict whose hotshot lawyer got him a gnu trial.

CRAZY QUESTION: Do postal police follow the letter of the law?

* * * * * * * * * * * * * * * * * *

Knock! Knock!
Who's there?
Sybil.
Sybil who?
Sybil court is different than criminal court.

* * * * * * * * * * * * * * * * * * * *

WHY DID MR. NOSE GET CONVICTED?

A WITNESS PICKED HIM OUT OF A LINEUP.

* * * * * * * * * * * * * * * * * * * *

What did the tape measure say to the lawyers? I'll give you my ruling tomorrow.

Guilty!

* * * * * * * * * * * * * * *

What do you get if you cross an IRS agent and a state policeman from Dallas?
A taxes ranger.

WHAT DID THE JUDGE SAY TO LAWYER CROW?
CAW YOUR NEXT WITNESS.

**Why does it take a convict so long to write a book?
Because sometimes they take ten years to complete a single sentence.**

What's the most difficult part of being a policeman at a nudist camp?
Finding a place to pin on your badge.

A ROBBER RAN INTO A DINER AND SAID TO THE CASHIER, "GIVE ME ALL OF YOUR MONEY."
THE CASHIER REPLIED, "YES, SIR. WILL YOU COUNT IT HERE OR IS THIS AN ORDER TO GO?"

What happened to the funny gangster?
He got riddled with bullets.

Gino: My uncle is in jail because he made big money.
Dino: How big?
Gino: About a quarter of an inch too big.

Auto Mechanic: Gulp! What do you want from me?
Robber: About a $1,000 and that's just an estimate.

Crook: Give me fifty bucks or else.
Rich Guy: I'm sorry, but I don't have fifty bucks. Can you break a $100 bill?

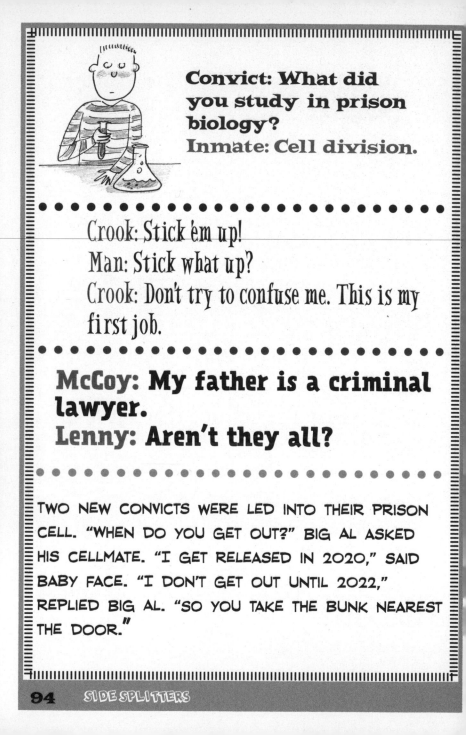

Convict: What did you study in prison biology?
Inmate: Cell division.

Crook: Stick 'em up!
Man: Stick what up?
Crook: Don't try to confuse me. This is my first job.

McCoy: My father is a criminal lawyer.
Lenny: Aren't they all?

TWO NEW CONVICTS WERE LED INTO THEIR PRISON CELL. "WHEN DO YOU GET OUT?" BIG AL ASKED HIS CELLMATE. "I GET RELEASED IN 2020," SAID BABY FACE. "I DON'T GET OUT UNTIL 2022," REPLIED BIG AL. "SO YOU TAKE THE BUNK NEAREST THE DOOR."

What do you get if you cross a policeman with a clock?
A crime watch.

What do you call a robber who lives next door?
The neighbor-hood.

COULD I STEAL A CUP OF SUGAR?

WHAT DOES A POLITE CONVICT SAY TO EVERYONE?
PARDON ME.

Nicky: Did you go to the Gangsters' Convention in Atlantic City?

Mickey: Yeah. It was a real mob scene.

What did the girl say after the gangster flirted with her?

I've been hoodwinked.

****

What did the gangster say when he saw the picture of a bank robber on the wall?
It's crooked.

Lawyer: Aren't you known as Mr. Groundhog? Is Mr. Groundhog your real name?
Attorney: I object, your honor. Counsel is badgering the witness.

CHAPTER

6

Funny Folks

What cartoon character lives in a marsh in Scotland?
Sponge Bog Square Pants.

* * * * * * * * * * * * * *

What cartoon character keeps a diary on the internet?
Sponge Blog Square Pants.

* * * * * * * * * * * * *

Who makes sure Sir Lancelot and his friends do not break curfew?
The knight watchman.

* * * * * * * * * * * * * * * * *

WHAT DO YOU GET IF YOU SMEAR JAM ON A PIRATE FLAG?
THE JELLY ROGER.

Knock! Knock!
Who's there?
Alma.
Alma who?
Alma treasure is buried on a desert island.

* * * * * * * * * * * * * * * * * * *

Who sails the ocean blue and has fleas? The Old Sea Dog.

* * * * * * * * * * * * * * * * * *

HOW DID PINOCCHIO BECOME A REAL BOY?

WHITTLE BY WHITTLE.

* *
Where does Blackbeard keep his gym shoes?
In Davy Jones' locker.

Which pirate is a great fisherman?
Captain Hook.

What do you get if you cross
a boy who lives in Neverland with
a skillet?
Peter Frying Pan.

Which lizard was the first treasurer of the United States?

Salamander Hamilton.

****

WHAT DID PETER ORDER FROM THE
NEVERLAND I-HOP?
PETER PANCAKES.

Who was **Michael Jackson Soda Bottle?**
The king of pop.

* *

When does Tarzan stop swinging through the trees?
When he reaches the finish vine.

• •

WHO LIVES IN NEVERLAND AND TELLS SILLY JOKES?
PETER PUN.

• •

Why did Pinocchio break up with his girlfriend?
She was stringing him along.

Who's in charge of the Neverland
Fire Department?

Captain Hook and Ladder.

• •

WHY DIDN'T NOAH DO ANY FISHING
ON THE ARK?

BECAUSE HE ONLY HAD TWO WORMS.

• •

**Why did Robin Hood's men hate
living in the woods?**

Sherwood Forest only had one
little john.

• •

**What lumberjack was an
All-Star player for the
Atlanta Braves?**

Woodchipper Jones.

WHO WEIGHS TWO TONS AND WENT TO THE BALL IN GLASS SLIPPERS? CINDERELEPHANT.

• • • • • • • • • • •

What do you call a big lumberjack with sore feet?
Paul Bunion.

• •

Why did Sir Lancelot remove his heavy armor?
He wanted to be a knight light.

• •

Who was the most famous sports rooter in China?
Cheerman Mao.

WHO CARVES WOODEN FIGURES AND LIVES UNDER THE SEA?

THE WHITTLE MERMAID.

What caped crime fighter has a huge ego?
Bruce Vain.

What cartoon character is a senior citizen?

Don Old Duck.

WHAT'S GREEN AND PECKS ON TREES?

WOODY WOODPICKLE.

What did Mickey Mouse say to his girlfriend on her birthday?
Minnie Happy Returns.

What did Bugs Bunny say to his girlfriend.
on her birthday?
Many hoppy returns.

What frog hero died at the Alamo?
Davy Croakett.

What do you get if you cross the Grand Canyon with American's first president?
Gorge Washington.

Teacher: Who is your favorite author?

Boy: SpongeBob.

Teacher: SpongeBob is a cartoon character. He never wrote any books.

Boy: That's why he's my favorite.

What did the Sasquatch eat for lunch?
A big foot long sandwich.

* * * * * * * * * * * * * *

What kind of vehicle does Mickey Mouse's girlfriend drive?
A Minnie van.

* *

KING ARTHUR: MOUNT YOUR STEED. WE'RE GOING TO KILL AN EVIL DRAGON.
SIR MORDRED: YAHOO! A SLAY RIDE.

* *

What do you get if you cross a zombie and Sir Lancelot?
The Dead of Knight.

Pirate #1: How did you get that new ship?
Pirate #2: We found it on sale.

Knock! Knock!
Who's there?
Scooby Doo.
Scooby Doo who?
Scooby Doo your homework right now.

PORKY PIG TOOK KARATE LESSONS. HE'S A HAM-TO-HAM COMBAT EXPERT. HIS PORK CHOPS ARE DEADLY BLOWS THAT LEAVE OPPONENTS BACON FOR MERCY.

What did Cinderella Seal wear to the ball?
Glass flippers.

How does a mermaid call her boy friend?
She uses her shell phone.

● ● ● ● ● ● ● ● ● ● ●

What did Mickey do when Minnie fainted?
He gave her mouse-to-mouse resuscitation.

● ● ● ● ● ● ● ● ● ● ● ● ● ● ●

Ed: Did Donald leave the party early?
Fred: Yes. He ducked out.

● ● ● ● ● ● ● ● ● ● ● ● ● ● ● ● ● ● ●

WHAT DO SMOKEY THE BEAR AND ALEXANDER THE GREAT HAVE IN COMMON?
THEY BOTH HAVE THE SAME MIDDLE NAME.

What did Bugs Bunny say to the pier?
What's up, dock?

What happened when Tarzan saw Jane?

He went ape over her.

DOES TARZAN DO BUSINESS IN HIS TREE HOUSE?
NO. HE HAS A BRANCH OFFICE.

Knock! Knock!
Who's there?
Tarzan.
Tarzan who?
Tarzan stripes are on the American flag.

Where does Tarzan work out?
At a jungle gym.

What does Tarzan the
Dairy Farmer swing on?

A bo-vine.

Which pig was an American president?
George Washingham.

Which stuffed
bear was an
American
president?
Teddy Roosevelt.

Which U.S. president hit a lot
of home runs?
Babe Lincoln.

Who was the devoted sidekick of the prehistoric Lone Ranger?
Tontosaurus.

WHAT DID KING KONG WEAR TO THE FORMAL DANCE?

A MONKEY SUIT.

What is Smokey's constitutional right?
He has the right to bear arms.

Dorothy: Tell me all about the Munchkins.
Witch Glenda: Sorry, I don't have time for small talk.

What do you get if you cross
Superman and bakery rolls?
Buns of steel.

* * * * * * * * * * * * * *

**WHAT DID SAILOR
SANTA SHOUT FROM THE
CROW'S NEST?
LAND HO HO HO!**

* *

**What does Mother Nature write on
during the fall?**

Loose-leaf paper.

How does the preamble to
the Munchkin Bill of Rights begin?
Wee the People.

WHAT DID THE NASTY KID SAY TO SPONGE BOB?

GO HOME AND SOAK YOUR HEAD.

* *

Why didn't Sponge Judy date Sponge Bill?
She thought he was too drippy.

• • • • • • • • • • • • • • •

What hobo lives in Neverland?
Peter Panhandler.

WILL
WORK
FOR
FAIRY
DUST

What does an angel say when it answers its cell phone?
Halo.

Boy #1: I heard Cupid almost got you last week.
Boy #2: Yes. I had an arrow escape.

ATTENTION: Atlas was the world's greatest crook. He held up the entire world.

WHAT DID THE LONE RANGER SAY AS HE SET THE TABLE?

HI HO SILVERWARE.

What knight outlived all the other members of the Round Table?
Sir Viver.

WHO CARRIES A BASKET TO GRANDMA'S HOUSE AND PENS BEST SELLERS?—LITTLE RED WRITING HOOD.

What kind of bread does Santa Claus like?

Ho-Ho-Wheat.

What did Captain Gretel shout to her crew?
All Hans on deck!

What did the NASCAR driver say when he had trouble steering his car?

I'm in wheel trouble.

CHAPTER

****7****

Food for Thought

What do you get if you cross a lighthouse and a chicken coop? Beacon and eggs.

WHAT DID THE FRUIT TREE SAY TO THE FARMER?
GO AND PICK ON SOMEONE ELSE.

Why did the fruit become a comedian?
It was berry funny.

Girl: I don't like this cheese with the holes in it.
Mother: Just eat the cheese and leave the holes on your plate.

Knock! Knock!
Who's there?
Micah.
Micah who?
Micah snack, I'm hungry.

MOM: WHEN MY SON BARRY FEELS SAD,
I ALWAYS BAKE HIM A PIE.

AUNT: IS IT A BLUE BARRY PIE?

* * * * * * * * * * * * * * * *

What noise does
Rice Chickies
cereal make?
Snap! Cackle! Pop!

* * * * * * * * * * * *

What's chewy
and makes up rhymes
to music?
A bubblegum rapper.

What does a skater use to slice bread?
A roller blade.

* * * * * * * * * * * * * *

WHAT DID ONE PLATE SAY TO THE OTHER?
LET'S BREAK FOR LUNCH.

****

What kind of health food goes down and then comes back up?
Yo-yogurt.

What do snobby vegetables do when they see poor farmers?
They turnip their noses.

NOTICE: High food prices are hard to swallow.

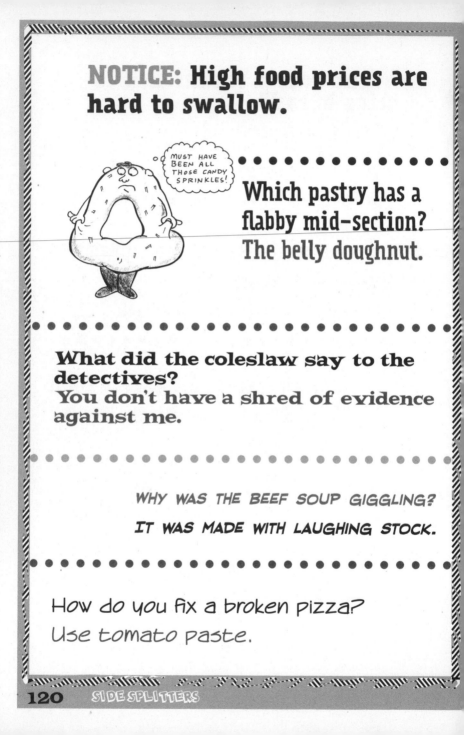

MUST HAVE BEEN ALL THOSE CANDY SPRINKLES!

Which pastry has a flabby mid-section?
The belly doughnut.

What did the coleslaw say to the detectives?
You don't have a shred of evidence against me.

WHY WAS THE BEEF SOUP GIGGLING?

IT WAS MADE WITH LAUGHING STOCK.

How do you fix a broken pizza?
Use tomato paste.

What grows on a fruit tree and repairs shoes?
An apple cobbler.

• •

WHAT IS THE MOST DANGEROUS
VEGETABLE TO HAVE ON A SAILBOAT?

A LEEK.

• •

Pancho: **Can I eat that?**
Cisco: **No. It's nacho cheese.**

• •

**What do you get if you
cross dogs and cheese?**
Mutts-a-rella.

• •

What kind of
sandwich does an
interrogator eat?
Grilled cheese.

Boy: There are two things I never eat for breakfast.
Girl: What are they?

Boy: Lunch and dinner.

▲▲▲▲▲▲▲▲▲▲▲▲▲▲▲▲▲▲▲▲▲▲▲▲▲▲▲▲

WHY IS IT BAD TO WRITE A LETTER ON AN EMPTY STOMACH?

BECAUSE IT'S MUCH BETTER TO WRITE ON PAPER.

▼▼▼▼▼▼▼▼▼▼▼▼▼▼▼▼▼▼▼▼▼▼▼▼▼▼▼▼▼▼

What do you get if you cross barley wheat and corn with country music? The Grain Ol' Opry.

THE HAY-SEEDS

▲▲▲▲▲▲▲▲▲▲▲▲▲▲▲▲▲▲▲▲▲▲▲▲▲▲▲▲

Why doesn't the Abominable Snowman celebrate Thanksgiving?
He quit cold turkey.

WHAT DID THE FARMER YELL TO THE
FIELD OF LETTUCE AT HARVEST TIME?

HEADS UP, EVERYONE!

What does a peanut become when it sneezes?
A cashew!

FAMOUS CHEFS:

I. Noah Recipe	Bern D. Stake
Ken I. Cook	Link Sausage
Hugh Etta Finemeal	Sal Idd
Seth D. Table	Al Mike Moore
Francie Foods	Frank Footer
Dot S. Goode	Will Dunne

Which vampire is always on a diet?
Count Calories.

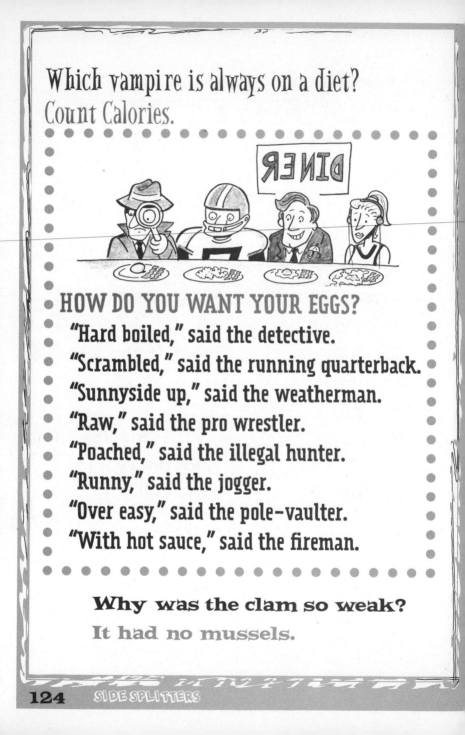

HOW DO YOU WANT YOUR EGGS?

"Hard boiled," said the detective.

"Scrambled," said the running quarterback.

"Sunnyside up," said the weatherman.

"Raw," said the pro wrestler.

"Poached," said the illegal hunter.

"Runny," said the jogger.

"Over easy," said the pole-vaulter.

"With hot sauce," said the fireman.

Why was the clam so weak?

It had no mussels.

NOTICE: A food scientist discovered how to duplicate dessert and now produces plenty of ice cream clones for everyone.

KNOCK! KNOCK!
WHO'S THERE?
GUT.
GUT WHO?
GUT MILK? I'M THIRSTY.

MR. PEAR: **WHY ARE YOU GOING TO THE DOCTOR?**

MR. BANANA: **BECAUSE I'M NOT PEELING WELL.**

Why do sharks live in salt water?
Because pepper water makes them sneeze.

BLESS YOU!

Bill: Where did you learn to make such great ice cream desserts?

Jill: I went to Sundae school.

● ● ● ● ● ● ● ● ● ● ● ● ● ● ● ● ● ●

What do Munchkins use to make sandwiches?
Shortbread.

● ● ● ● ● ● ● ● ● ● ● ● ● ● ● ● ●

PATRON: WAITER, WILL MY PIZZA BE LONG?

WAITER: NO, SIR. IT WILL BE ROUND.

● ● ● ● ● ● ● ● ● ● ● ● ● ● ● ● ● ●

What's the best way to bake perfect buns?

Use a roll model.

● ● ● ● ● ● ● ● ● ● ● ● ● ● ● ● ●

Muskrat: **What did you have for dinner last night?**
Beaver: **A tree course meal.**

WHAT DO YOU CALL A BOOK ABOUT SQUASHED ORANGES?

PULP FICTION.

• • • • • • • • • • • • • • • • • • •

Why did the farmer only plant one type of fruit tree in his orchard?

Because he was plum crazy.

• • • • • • • • • • • • • • • • • • •

Mother: Would you like to help me fix dinner?

Daughter: I'm sorry, Mom, but I think your cooking is beyond repair.

• • • • • • • • • • • • • • • • • • •

Mother: Junior why are you holding a slice of bread over your head at the breakfast table?

Son: I want to propose a toast.

Ben: I can make a pumpkin roll.
Jen: Big deal. I can make an apple turnover.

HOW DOES A GIRAFFE SAVE MONEY ON FOOD?

ONE BITE GOES A LONG WAY.

What does an earthworm use to season its food?

Ground pepper.

Why did the cookie crumble?
Because its mother had been a wafer so long.

WHAT DID MRS. COFFEE POT SAY TO HER TEENAGE SON?

PERK UP YOUR CLOTHES.

Why did the farmer sprinkle salt and pepper on his field? It was planting season.

Why was Ms. Corn so happy? Her boyfriend finally popped the question.

What is the one thing farmers don't want to grow? Older.

SIGN ON AN HERB SHOP: Closed. Out of Season.

How do you win free pancakes for life?
Buy a waffle ticket.

* * * * * * * * * * * * * * *

Knock! Knock!
Who's there?
Zip.
Zip who?
Zip your zoup quietly.

* *

WHAT DID MRS.
SWISS CHEESE
SAY TO HER
NASTY SON?
YOU'RE A
HOLEY TERROR.

What do you get if you cross a
lemon with a short letter?
A sour note.

Man: How much are your bananas?
Grocery Clerk: A penny each.
Man: Great. I'll take ten.
Grocery Clerk: That will be ten dollars and ten cents.
Man: Hey! I thought you said bananas were a penny each.
Grocery Clerk: They are. The peels they come in are a dollar each.

What did the melon groom say to the melon bride?
We cantaloupe tonight.

* *

Where were the first chickens fried?

In Greece.

* * * * * * * * * * * * *

PATRON: WHY IS THERE A FLY IN MY WATER?
WAITER: I GUESS HE DOESN'T LIKE OUR SOUP.

PATRON: WAITER, THIS FISH STEAK ISN'T AS GOOD AS THE FISH STEAK I HAD HERE LAST WEEK.
WAITER: THAT'S ODD, SIR. IT'S CUT FROM THE SAME FISH.

What did one potato chip say to the other?

Let's go for a dip.

What did the hungry monk say to the hamburger? Out of the frying pan and into the friar.

WHY DO POSTMEN HAVE GOOD DIGESTION?

BECAUSE THE MEAL MUST GO THROUGH.

What is a rabbit's favorite frozen treat?
A hopsicle.

• • • • • • • • • • • • • • • • • • • •

Why do golfers like doughnut makers?
They admire people who can make a hole in one.

• • • • • • • • • • • • • • • • • • • •

How do you lace a vegetable shoe?
Use string beans.

• • • • • • • • • • • • • • • • • • • •

LADY: HOW MUCH FOR A SLICE OF SPONGE CAKE?
BAKER: IT'S 66 CENTS.
LADY: AND HOW MUCH FOR A SLICE OF UPSIDE-DOWN CAKE?
BAKER: 99 CENTS.

• • • • • • • • • • • • • • • • • • • •

Why did the bakery hire a fitness instructor?
To firm up their buns.

WHEN DO PEARS AND APPLES NEED TO WEAR HELMETS? WHEN THEY PLAY IN A FRUIT BOWL GAME.

Waiter: Would you like a table, sir?
Patron: No. I came here to eat, not to buy furniture.

Uncle Al: My wife went to cooking school and graduated with frying colors.

A boy went to see his doctor. He had a string bean in one ear and a cherry in the other. He had a strawberry stuck in one nostril and a pea in the other. "What's wrong with me, Doc," asked the boy. Replied the doctor, "You're not eating right, son."

CHAPTER

8

Tom Swiftlies

SO, WHAT'S A TOM SWIFTLY, ANYWAY?

✳✳✳✳✳✳✳✳✳✳✳✳✳✳✳✳✳✳✳✳✳✳✳✳✳✳✳

Good question. Tom Swift was the main character in a series of adventure novels for kids first written in the early 1900s. (Sort of like the Hardy Boys and Nancy Drew, but not as well known.) In some of the novels, the authors tried really hard not to use the word "said" without an adverb to go along with it. So instead of writing:

"We must hurry," Tom said.

They'd instead write: *"We must hurry,"* Tom said *swiftly.*

It wasn't long before people began creating puns in which the adverb not only described how Tom and others said something but also somehow became a play on words with what was being said. There are hundreds of Tom Swiftlies out there, and after you're done reading these, come up with some of your own.

"Don't shoot! I'll throw down my weapon," the criminal cried disarmingly.

"I HAVEN'T BEEN BOWLING WELL LATELY," THE MAN GROANED GUTTERLY.

* * * * * * * * * * *

"I haven't eaten much in three days," said the dieter hungrily.

"My axe is not dull," remarked the lumberjack sharply.

"WE'RE HEADED FOR ROUGH WATER," YELLED THE RIVER GUIDE RAPIDLY.

* *

"Hey Troll! I'm crossing your bridge," shouted the Billy Goat gruffly.

"I love to eat hotdogs," admitted the baseball fan frankly.

"THE CORRECT ANSWER IS EIGHTY-TWO," REPLIED THE STUDENT SMARTLY.

"Water! Water! Give me water!" gasped the thirsty man dryly.

"Go to the corner and turn right," said the lady directly.

"THE MAD DOCTOR DIDN'T GIVE ME A BRAIN," MUTTERED THE SAD MONSTER MINDLESSLY.

"Burn the witch!" shouted the mayor of Salem wickedly.

"You've been a bad boy today," said the evil spirit devilishly.

"This lemon-aide is too sour," said the man bitterly.

"I WANT TO BE A SHEPHERD WHEN I GROW UP," ADMITTED THE BOY SHEEPISHLY.

"I'm a mischievous spirit," said the little ghost impishly.

"I DON'T LIKE FROZEN YOGURT," SNAPPED JANE COLDLY.

"How do you stop a runaway horse?" shouted the rider woefully.

"THIS HAT COST $1,000," BOASTED THE MAN GRANDLY.

"I'm really in love," shouted Mr. Rabbit hoppily.

"I'M NOT PROUD OF WHAT I DID," SIGHED THE CROOK SHAMEFULLY.

"I've decided to change your test score, Tom," the teacher remarked.

"Is it time to turn the pancakes?" Tom asked flippantly.

"I HURT MY ANKLE AND CAN HARDLY WALK," SAID TOM LAMELY.

"I've been under water for two and a half minutes," said Tom breathlessly.

"This entire story sounds like a tragic fairy tale," said Tom grimly.

"I just cut myself with an electric saw," said Tom offhandedly.

"I'm late for a pressing engagement," said Tom steaming.

"LET'S HAVE CHICKEN AND LAMB CHOPS FOR DINNER," TOM CLUCKED SHEEPISHLY.

"Stop cracking your knuckles," Tom popped off.

"DON'T SKATE ON THAT THIN ICE," TOM CRACKED.

THIN ICE (TOLD YOU!)

"It's time for a sweet snack," Tom snickered.

"I want to be a banker," Tom said with interest.

* *

"I smell gas," Tom fumed.

• •

"KEEP YOUR DOG QUIET," TOM BARKED LOUDLY.

* *

"My baseball team needs a homerun hitter," said Tom ruthlessly.

• •

"I'M MAKING CHOCOLATE CAKE," SAID TOM DEVILISHLY.

* *

"I keep banging my head against the wall," said Tom bashfully.

• •

"Growing vegetables is very relaxing," sighed the Green Giant peas-fully.

* *

"Duh," said Tom stupidly.

"I've been laid off due to the recession," said Tom idly.

• •

"I got the lowest I.Q. score of anyone who took the test," said Tom mindlessly.

* *

"I JUST CAN'T SEEM TO PUT THOUGHTS INTO WORDS," SAID TOM INDESCRIBABLY.

• •

"This dangerous liquid will eat through walls," said Tom acidly.

* * * * * * * * * * * * *

"I think archery is an aimless sport," Tom said with a quiver.

* * * * * * * * * * * * *

"I love mountain music," Tom sang loftily.

• •

"I cut firewood for three hours," Tom said as he lumbered through the door.

"Light the lamp," said Tom wickedly.

"We're out of pumpernickel bread," said the baker wryly.

"I like making furniture," said the carpenter in a crafty tone.

"THIS IS THE END OF ME," TOM CONCLUDED.

"Quick! Blow on the fire's embers," Tom bellowed.

"WATCH OUT! THAT KIND OF TURTLE BITES," TOM SNAPPED.

"We're having pork tonight," said Tom as he licked his chops.

"Get your hotcakes!" Tom flapped.

CHAPTER **9**

Daffy Doctors & Nutty Nurses

What does a psychiatrist like to eat on a picnic? Southern Freud Chicken.

SNIFF JUST LIKE MY MOTHER USED TO MAKE!

SIGMUND'S

PATIENT: DOCTOR, I HAVE AN INFERIORITY COMPLEX.
DOCTOR: THAT'S RIDICULOUS. YOU'RE TOO SMART FOR THAT.
PATIENT: OH NO I'M NOT.

Doctor: How long have you had amnesia?
Patient: How long have I had what?

Lady: Doctor, my son thinks he's a submarine.
Doctor: Uh oh! He's in deep trouble.

Lady: Doctor, my husband makes me boiling mad.
Doctor: Just simmer down now.

Lady: Doctor, my daughter thinks she's a rubber band.
Doctor: Relax, she'll snap out of it.

LADY: DOCTOR, MY NEPHEW IS VERY SICK. HE THINKS HE'S A BASKETBALL.
DOCTOR: CALM DOWN. HE'LL BOUNCE BACK.

What's the name of the psychologists' union?
The United Mind Workers of America.

Then there was the baseball umpire who had outpatient surgery.

✳✳✳✳✳✳✳✳✳✳✳✳✳✳✳✳✳✳✳✳✳✳✳✳✳

LADY PATIENT: DOCTOR, I FEEL FAINT.
DOCTOR: IF YOU FEE FAINT NOW, JUST WAIT UNTIL YOU GET MY BILL.

✳✳✳✳✳✳✳✳✳✳✳✳✳✳✳✳✳✳✳✳✳✳✳✳✳✳✳✳✳

Knock! Knock!
Who's there?
Decode.
Decode who?
Decode in my nose is getting worse.

• •

Knock! Knock!
Who's there?
Breed.
Breed who?
Breed deep and say "aah."

WHERE DOES A RABBIT GO TO FIX A BROKEN BONE?

TO A HARE SETTER.

●●●●●●●●●●●●●●●●●●●●●●●●●●●

What kind of vitamin did the doctor recommend for the sick spider?
Vitamin Bee.

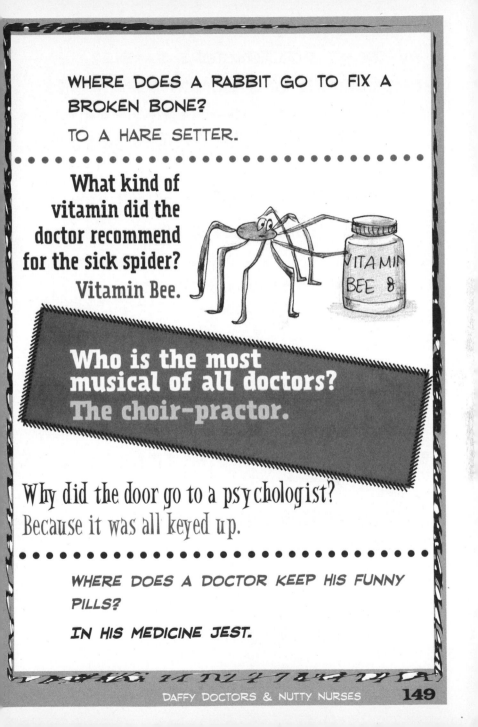

Who is the most musical of all doctors?
The choir-practor.

Why did the door go to a psychologist?
Because it was all keyed up.

●●●●●●●●●●●●●●●●●●●●●●●●●●●

WHERE DOES A DOCTOR KEEP HIS FUNNY PILLS?

IN HIS MEDICINE JEST.

WHY DON'T CHIROPRACTORS GAMBLE?
BECAUSE THEY ONLY BET ON SORE THINGS.

● ● ● ● ● ● ● ● ● ● ● ● ● ● ● ● ● ● ●

What did Dr. Crow say to say to his patient?
Take two aspirins and caw me in the morning.

● ● ● ● ● ● ● ● ● ● ● ● ● ● ● ● ● ● ●

If you're feeling sick and run down, sometimes visiting the doctor can prove to be a real shot in the arm.

● ● ● ● ● ● ● ● ● ● ● ● ● ● ● ● ● ● ●

THEY'RE A PERFECT MATCH. SHE'S A FAMILY DOCTOR ... AND HE MAKES EVERYONE SICK.

● ● ● ● ● ● ● ● ● ● ● ● ● ● ● ● ● ● ●

Zack: Why did you go to an eye doctor?
Mack: I was see sick.

● ● ● ● ● ● ● ● ● ● ● ● ● ● ● ● ● ● ●

What advice did the doctor give to the man who lived in a desert?
Get well soon.

Patient: Doctor, what's the quickest way to cure double vision?
Doctor: Shut one eye.

• • • • • • • • • • • • • • •

FATHER: MY DAUGHTER NEEDS BRACES.
DENTIST: WELL YOU'LL HAVE TO PUT YOUR MONEY WHERE HER MOUTH IS.

• •

Patient: **What's this prescription for?**
Doctor: **Tranquilizers.**
Patient: **When should I take them?**
Doctor: **Just before you look at my bill.**

• • • • • • • • • • • • • • • • • • • •

MR. JONES: WHY IS YOUR WIFE JUMPING ROPE?
MR. SMITH: BECAUSE THE DOCTOR TOLD HER TO TAKE TWO PILLS A DAY FOR A WEEK AND THEN SKIP A DAY.

Young Man: Doc, I don't dance, go to amusement parks, eat sweet desserts, or play video games. Do you think I'll live to be 100?

Doctor: You might if you don't die from boredom first.

****

MAN: WHAT'S UP, DOC?

DOCTOR: MY MALPRACTICE INSURANCE RATES.

● ●

DAFFY DEFINITION:
Dentist's Office — a filling station.

● ●

What does a doctor use to examine a lumberjack?

An axe-ray machine.

WHAT DO YOU GET IF YOU CROSS A COBBLER AND A DOCTOR? SOMEONE WHO HEELS SICK PEOPLE.

Knock! Knock!
Who's there?
Tamara.
Tamara who?
Tamara you'll feel better.

Knock! Knock!
Who's there?
Ally.
Ally who?
Alley did was check my temperature
and it cost me fifty bucks.

**What do you get if
you cross a patient
with a wheel?**
Someone who is
sick and tired.

I FEEL SO DEFLATED!!

Doctor: So, what's wrong with you?
Patient: That's what I'm paying you to tell me.

WHO TAKES CARE OF SICK LITTLE FISH?
THE SCHOOL NURSE SHARK.

Girl: How can I make my sick cat feel better?
Vet: Fill this purrscription.

WHAT DID THE DENTIST SAY TO THE DUCK?
BITE DOWN HARD.

Nurse: How is the little boy who swallowed the $100 bill?
Doctor: No change yet.

Lady: Doctor, my daughter thinks she's a stick of margarine.

Doctor: What do you want me to do?

Lady: Can you make her butter?

KNOCK! KNOCK!

WHO'S THERE?

EFFIE.

EFFIE WHO?

EFFIE FEELS BETTER, GIVE HIM SOME CHICKEN SOUP.

HOW DO YOU FEEL?

"I need to have my head examined," said Mr. Lettuce.

"I mashed my toes," said Mr. Potato.

"I feel run down," said Mr. Beet.

"I can't concentrate," said Ms. Orange.

ATTENTION: Bambi has a hart condition.

Patient: Doc, I have insomnia. What should I do?
Doctor: Try getting a little sleep.

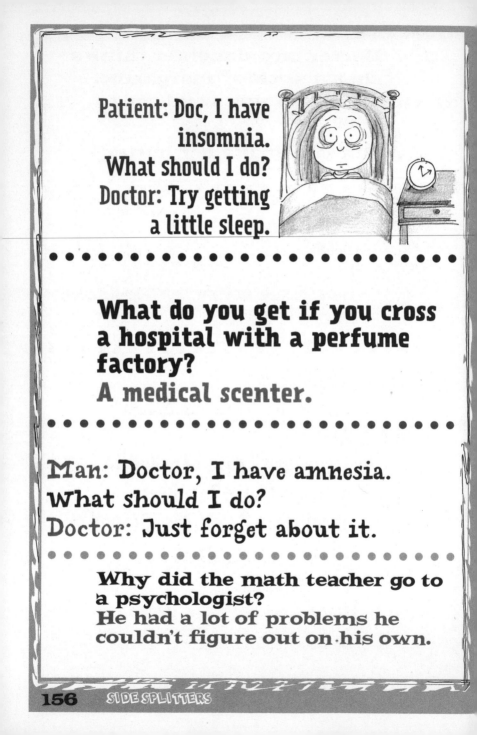

What do you get if you cross a hospital with a perfume factory?
A medical scenter.

Man: Doctor, I have amnesia. What should I do?
Doctor: Just forget about it.

Why did the math teacher go to a psychologist?
He had a lot of problems he couldn't figure out on his own.

SHOW ME A TRAINED
HYPNOTIST ... AND
I'LL SHOW YOU
A STARE MASTER.

• • • • • • • • • • • • • • •

Nurse: Take this
concentrated
lemon pill.
Patient: Why?
Nurse: It'll make you
feel bitter.

• • • • • • • • • • • • • • • • •

Doctor: What's wrong with you?
Patient: I swallowed a bone.
Doctor: Are you choking?
Patient: No doctor, I'm serious.

• • • • • • • • • • • • • • • •

**What is a podiatrist's
favorite song?**
There's no business like
toe business.

HARRY: I ALWAYS GET SICK THE NIGHT BEFORE I GO ON A TRIP.
LARRY: SO WHY DON'T YOU LEAVE A DAY EARLIER?

* * * * * * * * * * * * * *

KNOCK! KNOCK!
WHO'S THERE?
SIZZLE.
SIZZLE WHO?
SIZZLE HURT YOU MORE THAN IT HURTS ME.

* * * * * * * * * * * * * *

What did the cross-eyed teacher say to the eye doctor?
My pupils are out of control.

* * * * * * * * * * * * * * * * * * *

Girl: Who is the most famous baby doctor?
Boy: Who are you kidding? Babies can't be doctors.